Vol. 47, No. 5

Publisher, Patricia A. Pingry
Associate Editor, Nancy Skarmeas
Photography and Permissions Editor,
 Kathleen Gilbert
Contributing Editor, Bonnie Aeschliman
Art Director, Patrick McRae
Editorial Assistant, Fran Morley

ISBN 0-8249-1084-2

IDEALS—Vol. 47, No. 5 August MCMXC IDEALS (ISSN 0019-137X) is published eight times a year: February, March, May, June, August, September, November, December by IDEALS PUBLISHING CORPORATION, Nelson Place at Elm Hill Pike, Nashville, Tenn. 37214. Second-class postage paid at Nashville, Tennessee, and additional mailing offices. Copyright © MCMXC by IDE-ALS PUBLISHING CORPORATION. POSTMASTER: Send address changes to Ideals, Post Office Box 148000, Nashville, Tenn. 37214-8000. All rights reserved. Title IDEALS registered U.S. Patent Office.

SINGLE ISSUE—$4.95
ONE-YEAR SUBSCRIPTION—eight consecutive issues as published—$19.95
TWO-YEAR SUBSCRIPTION—sixteen consecutive issues as published—$35.95
Outside U.S.A., add $6.00 per subscription year for postage and handling.

The cover and entire contents of IDEALS are fully protected by copyright and must not be reproduced in any manner whatsoever. Printed and bound in U.S.A.

ACKNOWLEDGMENTS

THE JOY OF GETTING HOME from *HARBOR LIGHTS OF HOME* by Edgar A. Guest. Copyright 1928 by The Reilly & Lee Co. All rights reserved. Used by permission of the Estate; POTS AND PANS from *THE HEART CONTENT* by Douglas Malloch. Copyright 1926, 1927 by Douglas Malloch. Used by permission of the Estate; EARTH'S TREASURES from *HEART LEAVES* by Mamie Ozburn Odum. Copyright 1954 by Mamie Ozburn Odum. Used by permission; LAZY SUMMER DAYS from *AN OLD COPPER DIPPER* by Fannie Dee Pringle. Copyright 1963 by Fannie Dee Robinette Pringle. Used by permission; A HOME and A HOMEMAKER'S PRAYER from *AN OLD CRACKED CUP* by Margaret Rorke. Copyright © 1980 by Northwood Institute Press. Used by permission of the author; THAT MAKES A HOUSE A HOME from *MOMENTS OF SUNSHINE* by Garnett Ann Schultz. Copyright © 1974 by Garnett Ann Schultz. Used by permission. Our sincere thanks to the following whose addresses we were unable to locate: the Estate of Agnes Davenport Bond for HOME TO ME and SUMMER CAME from *HAPPY LANDING*. Copyright 1942 by Agnes Davenport Bond. All rights reserved; Maude Booth for MY ENCHANTED GARDEN; the Estate of Alice B. Dorland for SUSAN'S HOME from *ROAMING THE WIND*, Copyright 1955 by Alice B. Dorland; the Estate of Edna Greene Hines for WHERE THE HEART IS from *HARP OF THE PINES*; Minerva Kaarsberg for POETRY TO ME; Betty W. Stoffel for FOR THOSE WHO HAVE NO PLACE TO GO.

Four-color separations by Rayson Films, Inc., Waukesha, Wisconsin

Printing by Ringier-America, Brookfield, Wisconsin

The paper used in this publication meets the minimum requirements of American National Standard for Information Sciences—Permanence of Paper for Printed Library Materials, ANSI Z39.48-1984.

Cover by Dick Dietrich Photography
Kent's Corner, Vermont

The Harbor of Home

Caroline Eyring Miner

I thank Thee, Father,
    for my home,
A harbor calm where
    ships may come
To wait while angry
    tempests roll.
To keep this haven
    is my goal.

I do not wish
    to go abroad
To seek high honors
    men applaud,
Rare cargoes to make
    people stare.
I'll keep my home
    with faith and prayer.

Rockport Harbor
Rockport, Massachusetts
Ken Dequaine Photography

A Home

Margaret Rorke

Where two will toil together
   To make their human nest
Withstand life's windy weather
   And be a place of rest—

A center of affection
   Where children love and learn
And find in retrospection
   The truths to which they turn—

A bond of interweaving
   The all that touches each;
A trust, a true believing
   In everybody's reach—

A spell that's cast forever
   Upon the ones who roam,
For time and space can't sever
   The memory of a home.

Photo Opposite
Rose Arbor
Cape Cod, Massachusetts
Dick Smith, Photography

Summer Came

Agnes Davenport Bond

Summer came on gentle winds
With the fragrance she ensnares.
Trees now spread their leafy arms,
Bending with green she wears.

There is a hum of birds and bees,
Now the air is filled with song.
Bluest skies have foamy clouds
Drifting lazily along.

Shadows fall at evening tide,
Myriad stars are clear and bright,
As silently the darkness spreads
A dusky robe upon the night.

Linger summer, do not go.
You are hastening away.
All too soon these days will be
Memories of yesterday.

Photo Opposite
Little Colorado River
Near Greer, Arizona
Dick Dietrich Photography

The Heart Finds Home

Edna Greene Hines

A night's lodging and
A place to stay
Do not make a home.
An anchor there must be of
Old familiar scenes, old friends,
Old things lived with
That tie to the past.

Content and peace belong
To things long loved,
Though humble they may be:
Old books, old paths, old gardens,
And old loves.
In such as these
The heart finds home.

Photo Opposite
Elfreth's Alley
Philadelphia, Pennsylvania
Harold M. Lambert Studios, Inc.

Neighborliness

Craig Sathoff

Being a neighbor is many things,
But most important of all
Are the common everyday gestures,
The deeds we consider small.

The smile and wave from the porch steps,
Or the sample of fresh hot bread—
The postponement of a personal task
To help a neighbor instead.

The tangy pot of coffee
Ready to serve a guest—
The belief that one's friendships
Are the key to how much one is blessed.

Being a neighbor is many things.
But most important of all
Is the love and the thought behind the deed
Be it large or small.

Bennington, Vermont
Dick Dietrich Photography

Seven Gables Inn (1886)
Pacific Grove, California
Gay Bumgarner, Photographer

HOME TO ME

Agnes Davenport Bond

I have lived in stately halls
Where beauty was supreme,
Where all about, the loveliness
Fulfilled a happy dream.

I have traveled many miles,
Have slept upon the sea,
When cradled by the rolling waves
That tossed incessantly.

Floral Garden
Victoria, Canada
Gay Bumgarner, Photographer

I have camped in mountain wilds,
Nowhere to lay my head
Except within a canvas tent,
With pine boughs for a bed.

I have felt the desert winds
And breathed the desert air,
And found within its loneliness
A kindred peace to share.

I have loved these, one and all,
Wherever they might be,
And if I had my loved ones near;
They all were home to me.

Photo Overleaf
River Town
Fountain City, Wisconsin
Ken Dequaine Photography

The Simple Life

My life is quite confused
For I belong back years ago,
When things were quite simplistic,
Not the turmoil we now know.

There weren't new developments
Creeping up across the land,
But rather simple homesteads
Where the families farmed by hand.

There were no frozen foods
Or preservatives like now.
The foods were grown quite naturally
Or came from homegrown pigs and cows.

There weren't toys or gimmicks
Or things such as TV.
Handmade dolls or trucks or books
Would have been the only toys you
    might have seen.

Families were important
And the family structure made the home.
Everyone pitched in to do his share
No one person worked alone.

Oh yes, life was much more simple,
I wish I could have lived back then
Instead of in these frazzled modern days.
I'll sit and read and dream again . . .
Of when life was much more simple
In the good old days back when!

Janet E. Bedger
Akron, PA

Reflections

Home

Home is the place where heart meets heart,
Where kindly deeds abound,
Where gracious understanding reigns
And worlds of love are found.

Where, when the evening shadows come
And day has gone to rest,
We sit beside the fireside and count
    the ways we're blessed.

And home, the very word itself,
Brings courage and brings cheer,
Yes home is home because it holds
The things of life held dear.

Home is the roof above us, and
Though humble it may be,
We're rich indeed if love is there
And blessed beyond degree.

Rachel Zook
Quarryville, PA

Porch Swing

A hyperactive humming bee
Buzzes toward the hickory tree.
Birds are bustling after food,
But I am in a tranquil mood.
Sedated by the fragrant flowers,
Here I'll pass the summer hours,
Absorbing every summer thing,
Swinging in the old porch swing.

A butterfly decides to linger
On my very lazy finger,
As shadows tremble on the ground
From breezes blowing leaves around.
Perhaps you think I waste this day
In such a languid loafing way.
But dreaming in the old porch swing,
I'm at peace with everything.

Ericka Northrop
Tuscon, Arizona

BITS & PIECES

The domestic man, who loves no music so well as his kitchen clock, and the airs which the logs sing to him as they burn on the hearth, has solaces which others never dream of.

Emerson

Without hearts there is no home.

Byron

If a man be gracious to strangers, it shows that he is a citizen of the world, and his heart is no island, cut off from other islands, but a continent that joins them both.

Francis Bacon

A house without a roof would scarcely be a more different home, than a family unsheltered by God's friendship, and the sense of always being rested in His providential care and guidance.

Horace Bushnell

There is no place more delightful than one's own fireside

Cicero

Six things are requisite to create a "happy home." Integrity must be the architect, and tidiness the upholsterer. It must be warmed by affection, lighted up with cheerfulness; and industry must be the ventilator, renewing the atmosphere and bringing in fresh salubrity day by day; while over all, as a protecting canopy of glory, nothing will suffice except the blessing of God.

James Hamilton

Poetry

Minerva Kaarsberg

Poetry to me is this . . .
The softness of a baby's kiss,
The gentle voice that eases care,
The rhythm of the rocking chair,
The sunlight streaming through a door,
A kitten playing on the floor,
The colors in a silken shawl,
A shining mirror on the wall,
The time of day to sit awhile,
A dream that leaves one with a smile,
A house that hums . . . and beckons me
To step inside is poetry.

Photo Opposite
MacCallum House
Mendocino, California
Bob Clemenz Landscape Photograp

Thank God for Home

Grace Noll Crowell

I cannot thank Thee, God, enough
For this small plot of ground, this roof,
These lifted walls that close me in
And hold me tenderly; this proof
Of Thy kind care for my great need
Of shelter and of daily bread;
But oh, there are no written words,
There are no words that have been said
That could express my gratitude
For the companionship of love

That shares my simple fare—dear God,
A gift I would be worthy of!
And I would thank Thee for the tasks;
A fire to tend, a loaf to bake,
A floor to sweep, a seam to sew,
A clean, white-sheeted bed to make,
A lamp to light at evening time—
I thank Thee, God, for all of these:
For home, my home—for every home—
I thank Thee, God, upon my knees.

THANK GOD FOR HOME from the book *LIGHT OF THE YEARS* by Grace Noll Crowell.
Copyright © 1963 by Grace Noll Crowell. Reprinted by permission of Harper & Row, Pub-
lishers, Inc.

For a New Home

Alice MacKenzie Swaim

Blow gently, winds, around this house;
May happiness dwell here,
For these four walls contain the sum
Of all whom we hold dear.

May those who sit around our fire
Forget their load of care,

Rekindle dreams of heart's desires
As peace and joy they share.

Blow gently, winds; fall softly, rain,
And may a kind sun glow
And songbirds sing a sweet refrain;
May love and wisdom grow.

LAZY SUMMER DAYS

Fannie Dee Pringle

There is a certain serenity in late summer days,
    watching the concrete crawl along with its cargo
        of shimmering heat,
Vanishing with the day in the horizon haze;
    listening to the horseshoe repeat
        a ring made by an experienced pitcher.

Watching an old sea captain smoke his pipe and relate
    his rich experiences to bewildered children, who
Have docked their sailboats in the lily pond, with a
    passionate longing to recapture all the thrills and
        hardships the Captain went through,
Excitement shining in their eyes with
    immortal tenderness.

There is nothing beautiful, just simple and sweet,
    going out into the shade for a melon feed,
Watching Aunt Sue mark her Bible passage
    before the retreat,
Junior teaching his sister to spit out the seed;
    all common things, but something priceless
        in each one.

Glorious is the late summer day,
    nothing's more soothing than a late
        summer breeze;
It has a beauty all of its own the way
    it loosens yellow leaves and the way it teases
        and romps with the tumbleweed.

Photo Opposite
Bob Firth Photobank

A SLICE OF LIFE

Edgar A. Guest

The Joy of Getting Home

The joy of getting home again
    Is the sweetest thrill I know.
Though travelers by ship or train
    Are smiling when they go,
The eye is never quite so bright,
    The smile so wide and true,
As when they pass the last home light
    And all their wandering's through.

Oh, I have journeyed down to sea
    And traveled far by rail,
But naught was quite as fair to me
    As that last homeward trail.
Oh, nothing was in London town,
    Or Paris gay, or Rome
With all its splendor and renown,
    So good to see as home.

'Tis good to take these lovely trips,
    'Tis good to get away,
There's pleasure found on sailing ships,
    But travel as you may
You'll learn as most of us have learned,
    Wherever you may roam,
You're happiest when your face is turned
    Toward the lights of home.

Edgar A. Guest began his illustrious career in 1895 at the age of fourteen when his work appeared in the Detroit Free Press. *His column was syndicated in over 300 newspapers, and he became known as "The Poet of the People." Mr. Guest captured the hearts of vast radio audiences with his weekly program, "It Can Be Done" and, until his death in 1959, published many treasured volumes of poetry.*

Photo Overleaf
Sonoma, California
Ed Cooper Photo

WELCOME
HOME

John
Slobodnik

THROUGH MY WINDOW

Pamela Kennedy

Home—Handle with Care

Mama! Mama!" The excited voice of my six-year-old daughter reaches me, echoing around the stacks of boxes and off the barren walls.

"In here," I answer.

She rushes in, eyes sparkling, disheveled pigtails bouncing. Her face is smudged with dirt and her grubby hands cradle something with youthful tenderness.

"Look Mama, a bird's nest! I found it on the ground under the big tree. Maybe the bird family is moving too." She carefully deposits the treasure of grass and fibers in my hands, plants a kiss on my cheek, and skips back outside. "I'm going to see if I can find anything else," she calls over her shoulder. "Will you keep it for me?"

I sit in the rocker and examine the nest. The movers are due in an hour and there isn't anything else to be done now. The house is stripped of curtains and rugs. Dishes, toys, and books are packed in boxes; furniture waits to be loaded onto the trucks.

For the first time in weeks, it seems, I have time just to sit. Turning the little bird nest over in my hands I wonder at its simplicity. Our home seems such a complex mix of things, so difficult to define, but here in my hand rests a picture of all that is necessary and good about a home.

The mother bird instinctively knows to make her home circular in design. The sides rise up protectively, keeping out wind and rain from any direction, sheltering the little bird family from unfriendly forces. Just what a home should be, I think: a haven from the storms of life, somewhere safe where unkind winds and critical rains cannot bother us or bring us harm.

Soft feathers line the little hollow, comforting the bird babies like a gentle hug, no doubt. The mother has left bits of herself to warm her nestlings. I look again at the boxes stacked around me. In them are counted cross-stitch hangings, stuffed dolls, hand-made overalls, pinafores, tablecloths, and pillows. Like the mother bird, I have also "feathered my nest" with parts of myself, surrounding my family with tangible touches of love.

How intricately it is woven! Little bits of string and of grass, threads and shreds of abandoned fabric and fluff all intertwined to form a pattern from their randomness. I think again of our family and home. So many random acts and words, bits and pieces, scraps of experiences woven together, day by day, year by year, to create the tightly knit fabric of our home. Simple, yet complex; single, yet formed from many colored fragments—our nest is just a larger, bulkier version of this mother bird's home.

Anchored to the family tree, our nest sways and occasionally threatens to dislodge in the winds of argument and grief. Yet stronger than the bonds of straw that held this tiny nest in place, the bonds of love, of hope, and of commitment to each other hold us fast.

In the distance I hear the rumble of the moving van. Soon strangers will number all of our boxes, count our valuables, and haul them off. I will set up housekeeping somewhere else, hang my treasures on new walls, and store my memories in unfamiliar cubbyholes. But before long that house will lose its foreign feel and earn the title, "Home".

"Come in!" I call as the burly mover rings my bell.

He enters with his clipboard, checks his orders, and looks around.

"O.K. We'll start in here," he says. "Is there anything that needs special care or handling?"

I begin to shake my head, then change my mind. I place the bird's nest in his calloused hand and smile. "This," I say, "needs extra-special care."

Pamela Kennedy is a freelance writer of short stories, articles, essays, and children's books. Married to a naval officer and mother of three children, she has made her home on both U.S. coasts and currently resides in Hawaii. She draws her material from her own experiences and memories, adding bits of imagination to create a story or mood.

EARTH'S TREASURES

Mamie Ozburn Odum

When shall man learn earth's treasures
Are not gold, silver, or myrrh,
Or "things" that clutter up the home
Or worldly passions stir?

When shall man find earth's treasures—
Etched in the heart of a rose,
Soft cool rain, evening's breezes,
Or a baby's repose,

A golden sun sinking to rest,
Shade from a spreading tree,
A mellow-throated Mocker's song
Trilling glad and free?

Here man shall find earth's treasures—
In quiet familiar lanes,
Gold white light in early night
Outlining the window panes,

Childish voices free from care,
Sweet rest in the evening's gloam.
'Tis here treasures are waiting—
Carved deep in heart and home.

Photo Opposite
Phlox and Geraniums
Gay Bumgarner, Photographer

FROM MY
G·A·R·D·E·N
JOURNAL

Deana Deck

Cool, Clear, Water Gardens

On the hottest days of summer, nothing can lend a cooling touch to the environment as effectively as a small pool, shimmering with light and shadow, and graced with delicate blossoms floating on its surface.

Many people equate such garden pools with the formal structures found on the lawns of state-

ly mansions. It's understandable. The great gardens of Europe were frequently centered on spectacular water features—fountains and lily pools in French chateaux; elegant, formal Victorian pools; and the reflecting pools found in Italian villas. This lingering image of aristocratic grandeur, along with the common belief that waterlilies are difficult to grow, has kept pools and ponds out of the average homeowner's garden. This is unfortunate; waterlilies have been on the planet for over 120 million years, and while they certainly have been the center of many exotic garden designs, the plants themselves have simple needs and will thrive in the most unpretentious backyard pools.

Slowly, however, the public conception of waterlilies is beginning to change, thanks to the recent proliferation of inexpensive, prefabricated pools of fiberglass, plastic, and stone, and the appearance of the plants themselves in more and more mail order catalogues. Today dozens of companies exist, anxious to supply easy-to-grow aquatic plants, many small enough to be grown in a tub on a balcony.

Prefabricated pools are appealing because they are ready-to-use, but by adapting other containers or constructing your own, you can have the perfect pool for much less.

The simplest and least expensive way of creating your own pool is to scoop out a shallow hole in the corner of your yard—three feet or so in diameter—and line it with heavy black plastic. Disguise the edges with attractive stones from a nearby creekbed, set a few potted ferns at the corners, and you have created a piece of instant serenity.

A larger pool is created in much the same manner, with a few extra precautions. Make sure to level the bottom of the hole carefully, to prevent debris from collecting in small pockets, and to cover the bottom with a thick, cushioning layer of sand to protect the liner from perforations. Line a larger hole with the seamless, heavy-gauge plastic used by roofing contractors.

Before filling the pool, anchor the edges securely with large stones, then slowly run in water. As the pool fills, loosen the stones to allow the liner to slip and settle snugly into curves and crevices. Once the pool is full, replace the stones, or add bricks or a similar decorative edging. After the waterlilies are in place, consider adding a few goldfish. They not only add color and life to your water garden, but they will help keep the pool clean!

If you have no room for a large pool, other containers can be pressed into service to create a miniature water garden. On a balcony, even a Chinese wok or the basin of an attractive birdbath can provide a home for an aquatic plant or two. A half barrel of the sort used for planters is adequate to support a full-sized waterlily year round.

A little known fact about waterlilies is that many species are hardy in winter, some as far north as Zone 3. If your pool is at least two feet deep, the hardy varieties can survive under ice all winter, going dormant in fall as the weather cools. These perennial waterlilies bloom from about May until September in northern climates, and from April to November in southern gardens.

One of the best varieties of waterlily with which to start, especially in a small pond, is the white Marliac, or Marliac Albida, a fragrant, prolific bloomer. If you like color, you are in luck, because waterlilies are wonderfully colorful, even when they are not in bloom. The foliage is a burgundy color on the underside, and the leaves usually curl a bit to reveal this surface. The edges are tinted red and some plants have variegated green and burgundy surfaces.

The waterlily's flowers are usually either white, yellow, or shades of pink and apricot. One variety, the Cherokee, starts yellow and fades to white. The Attraction variety starts pink, but by the third day has changed to red. Most varieties are day-bloomers, but if you are away all day, consider purchasing a night-blooming variety instead. It will be opening just about the time you get home, and you can admire it all through the evening.

Don't let the task of building a pool discourage you; a backyard water garden is worth the initial work. When the heat of the summer is at its peak, you will be thankful for the cool, refreshing, colorful sight of floating waterlilies in bloom, and throughout the year, you will be amazed at the ease of maintaining this bit of private serenity.

Deana Deck lives in Nashville, Tennessee, where her garden column is a regular feature in the Tennessean.

TRAVELER'S *Diary*

Marian H. Tidwell

Geraniums in the foreground of the Garden's gallery of Boehm porcelain.

One of the World's Most Beautiful Gardens

In 1918, Walter Bellingrath purchased over 900 acres of land along the Fowl River in Theodore, Alabama, just south of Mobile. Mr. Bellingrath was an avid fisherman; and he looked to this land, with its many lakes and ponds, as a private haven for relaxation and recreation—an escape from the pressures of his day to day life as owner of a cola bottling company.

But Bellingrath's wife, Bessie, had other plans for the land. Her interest was in plants and gardening; for Mrs. Bellingrath, the acquisition of so much new land was an invitation to expand and develop this hobby into a full-time pursuit. And Mrs. Bellingrath's enthusiasm proved contagious—it was not long before her husband too

was consumed by the notion of turning the land into a grand garden. Together, they gathered plants of all varieties from all over the country and brought them home to Theodore.

As the garden grew in size and scope, word spread through the area that the Bellingraths had created something spectacular. In April of 1932, the Bellingraths responded to public interest and opened their garden to the community. The story goes that the crowds were so large that first day that the local sheriff's department had to help keep order; whether or not this is true, the Gardens were an instant success with the public, and remain so today.

At the center of the Gardens stands the Bellingrath home, which was built between 1935 and 1936 of antebellum brick gathered from a torn-down hotel in Mobile. The seventeen rooms now hold Mrs. Bellingrath's collections of furniture, china, porcelain, and glassware. The house, like the Gardens themselves, has been listed on the National Register of Historic Places.

The upkeep of the Gardens and the home is provided for by the Bellingrath-Morse Foundation, which was established with the fortune that the Bellingraths accumulated in their cola business. This generous funding pays the large staff of professional gardeners who ensure that the grounds are well-maintained in all four seasons. And Bellingrath does have flowers for each of those seasons. In late spring and early summer, the Gardens are at their peak, with allamanda, salvia, roses, hibiscus, copper plants, and much more. From September to February, the camellias line the garden walkways; and in late autumn and

Rustic bridge over Mirror Lake

an eight-minute presentation on the history of the garden and provides an update on the season's particular blooms.

Bellingrath Gardens have been called the most beautiful garden spot in the American southeast. They certainly live up to this grand praise. No matter what the season, Bellingrath has something in bloom. Still, quantity alone does not guarantee a beautiful garden; Bellingrath is wonderfully landscaped and is always meticulously maintained.

These gardens are definitely a spot for knowledgeable flower lovers; anyone who has ever grown a garden of his or her own will be impressed and amazed at the scope and beauty of Bellingrath. Yet this is also a place for those with little practical knowledge of gardening. Bellingrath is a delight whether one's aim is a quiet stroll or an educational tour.

After all these years, and all the work of the Bellingraths and the teams of professional gardeners who have tended the Gardens since 1932, Bellingrath Gardens are exactly what Walter Bellingrath had in mind when he first purchased the land—a quiet haven from the rush of the day-to-day world, a public place for the private sanctuary we all seek.

A view of the grotto with hydrangeas.

winter, multi-hued chrysanthemums explode in what has become the world's largest outdoor display of this favorite flower.

Indoors at Bellingrath there are horticultural exhibits centered upon the blooming plants in season—including a ten-foot high poinsettia tree during the holiday season. A small theater runs

The grotto with alamanda.

Why Bother to Have a Garden?

Wanda M. Read

Why do we bother with gardens, when good, fresh produce is always "in season"—and a bargain as well—at the supermarket? Why do we enslave ourselves, driven by the season and the need to get it tilled, then to get it planted, and finally to haul in the harvest in quantities determined by the garden and not by our own wishes?

We work to save our garden from sure death when rain is scarce, and to save it from strangulation when rain, and weeds, are ample. Then we endure steamy hours in the kitchen, canning and freezing, pickling and jelling—putting up the harvest—when it would be far more pleasant to be outdoors.

Why do we garden? Because it feels good to

us. Gardening felt especially good to my husband and me after a year of drought, when our tiller dug deep, but turned up only dust, and the soil lay fallow all summer long. Late rains were wasted, nurturing only a feeble stand of weeds to haunt us.

Gardening feels good now, after such a dry, fallow year. We planted early and watched for any signs of thirst. We mulched heavily, both to conserve precious moisture and to help hold our ground against the inevitable offspring of the previous year's weed cover.

Each garden is a new creation. We work it out on graph paper—flowers in each plot, double cropping, companion planting—always with an eye to height, to afternoon shade, and

38

to morning sun. Always, however, nature has the final say in what grows where, how much of it grows, and when it matures: beauty balances utility. Convenience of harvest would be nice, but usually everything comes at once, just as it always has.

Working in our garden, we stop to look out beyond our plots, to the grain fields around us and the woods beyond them.

"It's all ours," I comment. As far as we can see, as far as we can imagine, these are our foothills. No matter that we do not pay taxes on all of it or hold a deed to it. It is ours this day.

As we listen, we find that we are not alone. Robins bounce from cherry tree to grape arbor, bees zoom between cosmos and bean blossoms, each seeming to be tending a garden of his own. Near my resting feet, an ant hauls a

tiny stick over blades of grass and a small black beetle works at a clump of earth. As we go back to work, we are filled with new inspiration.

"We have made a good garden here," I say as I pinch suckers from a burgeoning tomato plant.

"Not us. We only planted it," my husband reminds me as he winds the lengthening tendrils of a stalk of Blue Lake beans around a newly set pole.

This is why we garden. It is a cooperative system. We work, we listen, we take direction; we share in the harvest.

"We assisted then, in making a good garden here." He agrees. We don't make a garden, and we don't simply take from its store. We are privileged, rather, to have a role in the process.

Grandma Is Coming

Elizabeth Page

Grandma is coming
To stay for a week.
She'll call me her "sweetness"
And tickle my cheek.
I can't wait to hug her
And nuzzle her face.
She smells just like powder
And sunshine and lace.

She says she'll find
Sugar on my neck.
She says she loves me
A bushel and a peck.
I know she'll bring me
Some new shoes to wear,
A dress that she made,
And a bow for my hair.

She'll dress me up
And I'll make a mess
But Grandma won't care
If I get stuff on my dress.
When Mom goes to work,
We'll dress up the cat
And have tea parties
And cuddle and chat.

She'll let me ride
The horse on her lap.
Then lie down beside me
While I take my nap.
Grandma just laughs
At all that I do.
She counts all my piggies
And wiggles them, too.

She knows where
My ticklish places are.
I can't wait to see her
Drive up in her car.
I'll wait at this window
Until I can see
Mommy's mommy
Smiling at me.

Grandma's Coming by Donald Zolan

© Pemberton & Oakes. All rights reserved.

41

Country CHRONICLE

—— Lansing Christman ——

Henry Thoreau knew intimately the value of building a home in harmony with the outdoor world. He built his cabin in the woods, near Walden Pond, and for two years he lived there alone. In his book *Walden* he tells why:

I went to the woods because I wanted to live deliberately, to front out the essential facts of life, and see if I could not learn what it had to teach, and not, when I came to die, discover that I had not lived. I did not wish to live what was not a life; living is so dear.

We, too, live this life close to nature. Our home is a simple dwelling, situated on a gentle knoll among the rolling hills. From here, we can

look down the valley, or to higher hills and mountainsides. Pastures and fields unfold before us; orchards and woodlands stretch out toward a ravine and its meandering stream.

We have nature at our doorstep. The rabbits come up from the thicket on summer evenings to nibble on clover leaves by the walk. Bees hum in the daytime as they sip nectar from the blooms. Birds come to the trees; butterflies and humming-birds come to the flowers by the door.

Here, I am content. By day there is the glory of the sun; then comes twilight, and the dark of night. These are enchanting hours. We sit in chairs on the lawn, listening to the crickets' music from dooryard and garden. We hear the tinkling of cowbells from a far-off pasture slope. Stars begin to glisten in the sky like jewels in the heavens. This tranquil mood of twilight fills our hearts with a love of God, of nature, and of life itself. Here, we are at home.

The author of two published books, Lansing Christman has been contributing to Ideals *for almost twenty years. Mr. Christman has also been published in several American, foreign, and braille anthologies. He lives in rural South Carolina.*

My Enchanted Garden

Maude G. Booth

The path is set with polished jade,
The fence, a string of crystal pearls.
A silver gate with crystal burls
And chairs of rose-hued silk brocade.

A pixie holds the lamp post true,
A beetle taps his tune between
White clover on the carpet's green
As laughing bluebirds sip the dew.

I've leased it all to fairyfolks
Who romp each fragrant summer night
Till twinkling stars have taken flight
Then scamper back to woodland oaks.

Photo Opposite
Gay Bumgarner, Photographe

Grandma's Aprons

Harriet Whipple

I recall the kind of aprons
That Grandma used to wear;
She seldom was without one,
Starched and ironed with care.

They either were of gingham checks
Or flowered dark percale—
She choose the cloth to make them
Herself from the goods on sale.

She always made them just alike,
Each bound with matching tape,
She often cut the pockets
A different size or shape.

Her aprons saved her dresses,
And they had other uses too,

Like bringing in some ripened plums
Or the vegetables she grew.

Her apron made a handy fan
When days were extra warm,
And it carried in the laundry
When there came a sudden storm.

She would use it for a holder
If handles got too hot,
Or to flick away a bit of dust
On some conspicuous spot.

Her apron was a uniform
For a busy grandma to wear—
A part of her image I always recall
Along with the loving care.

It only hung behind the door
When she had gone away,
And I see her in her apron still
Within my heart today.

PRESERVING SUMMER'S BOUNTY

When gardens and orchards are producing an abundance of fresh vegetables and fruit, it's time to preserve some of that goodness to enhance winter meals. Our recipes are delightfully different, bursting with flavor, and beautiful too! These recipes make wonderful gifts from your kitchen—you might want to make an extra batch for your family and special friends.

Italian Tomato Wedges

5   pounds tomatoes
1/2 pound Vidalia onions, thinly sliced
2   sweet green peppers, sliced into 1/4-inch
      strips
5   teaspoons Italian seasoning
1 1/2 teaspoons parsley

Prepare home canning jars and lids according to manufacturer's instructions. Peel, core, and quarter tomatoes. In a large stock pot combine tomatoes, sliced onions, and pepper strips. Bring to a boil and boil 5 minutes. Pack into hot jars, leaving 1 inch head space. Add 1 teaspoon Italian seasoning and 1/4 teaspoon parsley to each jar. Cover with boiling water, leaving 1 inch head space. Remove air bubbles. Adjust caps. Process 30 minutes at 10 pounds pressure in pressure canner.

Yield: about five pint jars.

Herbed Carrots and Green Beans

10   pounds fresh green beans
2   pounds small carrots
1 1/2 teaspoons marjoram leaves
1 1/2 teaspoons rosemary leaves
1/2 teaspoon parsley flakes
1/2 teaspoon white pepper

Prepare home canning jars and lids according to manufacturer's instructions. Wash and snap beans. Wash, peel, and slice carrots into 1-inch julienne strips. In large stock pot combine carrots and green beans. Add enough water to cover. Bring to a boil and boil 5 minutes. Drain vegetables. Pack into hot jars, leaving 1 inch head space. To each jar add the following: 1/4 teaspoon rosemary leaves, 1/8 teaspoon parsley flakes, 1/8 teaspoon white pepper. Carefully pour boiling water over vegetables, leaving 1 inch head space. Remove air bubbles. Adjust caps. Process 25 minutes at 10 pounds pressure in pressure canner.

Yield: about five quart jars.

Summer Delight

7   pounds peaches
2   fresh pineapples
1   cantaloupe
1 1/2 pounds cherries
4 1/2 cups cranberry juice
7   cinnamon sticks

Prepare home canning jars and lids according to manufacturer's instructions. Peel, pit, and quarter peaches. Soak in solution to prevent darkening. Pit cherries; set aside. Halve cantaloupe and remove seeds. With a melon baller, scoop out cantaloupe or cut into 1-inch cubes; set aside. Pare pineapple, remove eyes, and core. Cut into 1-inch wedges.

   Pour cranberry juice into stock pot and bring to a boil over medium high heat. Reduce heat. Fill large stock pot half full with water. Place over high heat and bring to a boil. Drain peaches. Place a small amount of each fruit in wire basket and lower into water. Simmer 3 to 5 minutes. Drain fruit and pack into hot jars, leaving 1/2 inch head space. Repeat until all jars are full. Add 1 cinnamon stick to each jar. Carefully ladle hot juice over fruit, leaving 1/2 inch head space. Remove air bubbles. Adjust caps. Process 20 minutes in boiling water bath canner.

Yield: about seven 1 1/2-pint jars.

Bonnie Aeschliman is a teacher of occupational home economics and a freelance food consultant. She lives in Wichita, Kansas, with her husband and their two children.

48

Photo courtesy of B

A HOMEMAKER'S PRAYER

Margaret Rorke

Dear Lord, who once brought forth the food
To feed a hungry multitude,
Forgive the grumbling you survey
When I prepare three meals a day.

O Lord, who cleansed from man his sin,
Give strength to me as I begin
To wash the dishes, clothes, and floors
And do my countless household chores.

O Lord, who asked the children near,
Bless those I love and hold most dear.
Put patience in my teaching too
Until in thought they come to You.

O Lord, who suffered untold pain,
Be merciful when I complain
About some little hurt I have.
Make love and faith its healing salve.

O Lord, who gave Your life to good,
Help me to help my neighborhood,
My church, my friends, and those who need.
Help me and mine to love Your creed.

O Lord, who left Your heavenly home
Because our Father bid You roam,
Make this, our dwelling, truly blest
By living with us as our guest.

COLLECTOR'S CORNER

Button Collecting

Brass button, 1890.

Are you the owner of your mother's or grandmother's button box, jar, or tin? Do you cut off the buttons from worn garments stashed away in your sewing basket, dresser drawers, or attic? If so, you are well on your way to becoming a button collector. Surprisingly, button collecting is now as popular as coin and stamp collecting.

No one knows for certain where the first button was made and worn, but we do know that ancient clothing fasteners were not buttons at all, but pins, girdles, brooches, buckles, and tie-strings. We can, however, find brass buttons on sixteenth-century dresses. *The Century Dictionary* of 1889 tells us that buttons were often sewn onto garments as ornaments and that in the eighteenth century, gentlemen at the French court sported buttons of gold, precious stones, pearl, and enamel.

Most collectors know that it is practically fruitless to search for buttons from before 1700. It was not until the eighteenth century that garment buttons became fashionable and were produced from gilt, silver, wood, pewter, brass, horn, and paper-mache. During the nineteenth century, but-tons were manufactured in England, France, Germany, and the United States. By 1850, there were fifty-nine button manufacturers in the United States alone.

Button collecting caught on as a hobby during the depression. Button collectors were featured on radio programs and since listeners had more time than money—and since most already owned buttons or had access to them cheaply—the hobby caught on and soon spread from coast to coast.

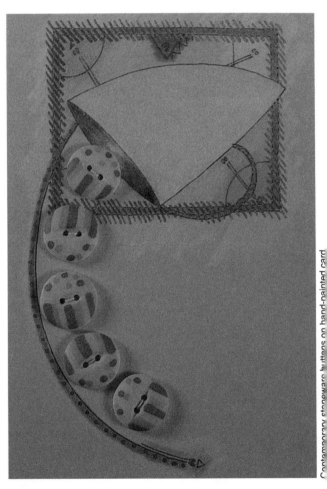

Contemporary stoneware buttons on hand-painted card.

52

In 1938, fifteen people gathered in Chicago to organize The National Button Society. Other state and local societies were formed soon after and continue to be organized around the world. Currently there are button collecting groups in at least thirty-two states, plus one in Washington, D.C. The hobby has become so popular that there is now a magazine devoted exclusively to button collecting, and there are also vast button collections in several museums and dealers who sell nothing but buttons. There's even an annual National Button Week in March.

Most buttons are still within the price range of the average collector, but prices are going up. A George Washington inaugural button, for example, can be priced at over $1,000. Still, avid collectors continue to find bargains. They shop at flea markets, garage sales, and charity shops to examine old clothing for rare finds to add to their collections. Some are also studying modern buttons and purchasing those they hope will increase in value in the years to come.

Still, no matter how popular button collecting becomes, and no matter how prices rise and spe-

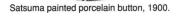

Satsuma painted porcelain button, 1900.

Painted ivory button, early 19th century.

Victorian gilded brass button, 1860.

Collectors are both generalists and specialists. Some concentrate on buttons manufactured before 1918; still others have a special interest, such as military, uniform, or work-clothing buttons. Collectors of "goofies," or realistic buttons, are fascinated with post-1935 buttons, usually of metal or of plastic, in recognizable shapes of fruits, vegetables, cars, and animals.

A new collector might be surprised to find hand-painted porcelain buttons, large jewel-filled Gay 90s buttons, buttons with Currier and Ives prints, ivory buttons in the shape of walruses and seals, heart-shaped or fruit-shaped buttons, or hard rubber buttons from the nineteenth century with the name of a rubber company on their backs.

Some button enthusiasts have found that buttons complement other collectibles. For example, collectors of teddy bears find themselves purchasing buttons shaped like their favorite stuffed animal; pewter collectors fall in love with buttons made from the same material; and collectors of Disney memorabilia seek Mickey Mouse and Donald Duck buttons.

cializations develop, it will always be a hobby available to all, as long as buttons remain a part of our wardrobes, and as long as our grandmother's button boxes remain tucked away on our shelves.

Victorian picture button, 1890.

Donna Paananen is a teacher and freelance writer who lives in East Lansing, Michigan. She collects everything from toys and dolls to postcards and old linens, and is the proud owner of her late mother's can of buttons.

Photos from the Tender Buttons Collection, New York.

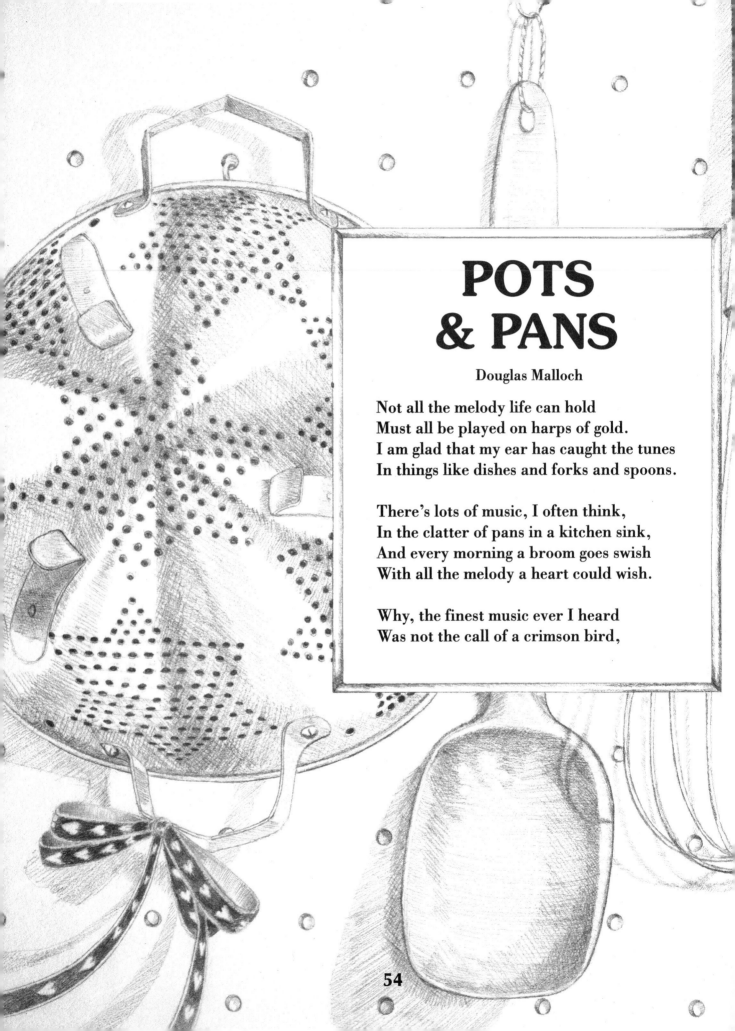

POTS
& PANS

Douglas Malloch

Not all the melody life can hold
Must all be played on harps of gold.
I am glad that my ear has caught the tunes
In things like dishes and forks and spoons.

There's lots of music, I often think,
In the clatter of pans in a kitchen sink,
And every morning a broom goes swish
With all the melody a heart could wish.

Why, the finest music ever I heard
Was not the call of a crimson bird,

But a peddler passed with a creaking van,
And I almost went with that roving man.

For his swaying pans and swinging pails
Rolled and rattled and ran the scales,
And filled my soul with their gypsy song
Till I nearly followed that van along.

The gypsy van dropped over the hill,
But it left its music behind it still.
I wipe the silver, I rattle the pans,
And I make a tune like that gypsy man's.

It's really remarkable what is in
A pot, a kettle, a plate of tin,
For the hand that works with a heart that sings
Finds many a tune in the commonest things!

Copyright © 1986 by Barbara Milo Ohrbach. Photographed by Joe Standart. Reprinted by permission of Clarkson N. Potter, Inc. An expanded version of this work appears in *THE SCENTED ROOM* by Barbara Milo Ohrbach.

CRAFTWORKS

Lavender Sachets

Selecting Fabrics for a Sachet

While many fabrics will make wonderful looking sachets, some will work better than others. I prefer fabrics made from natural fibers since they readily allow the scent of the sachet to escape into the air. These include cotton, linen, and silk. Even simple muslin, pillow ticking, or linen toweling can look pretty and fresh with the addition of a colorful ribbon.

Use patterns that are scaled to the size of the bag. Liberty florals, French wallpaper stripes, or small patterned chintzes are all good choices. Avoid very large prints.

Antique fabric scraps like small quilt pieces or bits of Victorian silk can be made into truly beautiful sachets. Pieces of handmade lace—old or new—lined with batiste or tulle in solid white or a soft pastel will always look special.

Interesting and pretty ribbons are a must and should be selected to coordinate with your fabrics. In fact, you can even make a sachet from the ribbon itself if it's 1½ inches wide or more.

Making a Sachet

Once you've collected your fabrics and ribbons, you're ready to start sewing. To make a very beautiful, nicely finished sachet, do the following:

1. Cut a rectangle of fabric that measures 8 x 11 inches.
2. Fold the fabric in half lengthwise, right sides together, and stitch down the long open side and one short side, using a ½-inch seam allowance.
3. Fold the top of the bag about halfway down over the bag itself and iron. (This piece will stay tucked into the bag when turned right side out.)
4. Turn the bag right side out and fill it two thirds full with potpourri mixture.
5. Tie it with an 18-inch length of ¼- or ½-inch wide ribbon, making a double knot and a bow.

Sachet Recipes

It doesn't matter if the ingredients of a sachet mixture get crushed in the blending because they'll be hidden inside the sachet rather than being on display in a container or a jar. Consequently, the directions are simple:

1. Mix all ingredients in a glazed pottery bowl.
2. Put the potpourri into a brown paper bag lined with wax paper and store in a cool, dark place for a period of two weeks. Occasionally stir the contents with a wooden spoon to disperse and blend the oils.
3. When the potpourri has "cured," spoon it into the fabric bags and tie with ribbon.

Lavender Sachets

This is one of my great favorites and also what I consider to be the simplest recipe to make. Since it has few ingredients, it can be quickly made.

It's an especially pleasing scent to find in a lingerie or handkerchief drawer, or in a box of writing paper. I put a sachet in each of my desk drawers and the paper, being an absorbent material, then takes on a light lavender scent.

Lavender flowers are very fragrant (even without the addition of the oils), so a nice bonus of this sachet is that it lasts a long time. In little print cotton bags, they'll look as fresh as they smell.

3 ounces lavender flowers
1 ounce powdered orrisroot
4 drops lavender oil

Yield: 4 ounces, or enough to make four sachets.

Barbara Milo Ohrbach.

57

I Remember When

Faye Field

When I was about to marry, my mother asked me if I wanted her old black iron skillet, which was too heavy for her to lift easily.

Of course I wanted it; when I held that iron skillet in my hand, a thousand memories filled my heart.

I remembered the crispy, succulent fried chicken served when we returned from church on Sundays; I remembered the spider corn bread that my mother dished out to feed the hungry workers in from the fields where they had been harvesting grain; and I remembered the mounds of freshly dug potatoes that fried so tender in that black iron pan.

I remembered standing and frying corn, straight from the garden on early June days.

Many of my dreams took shape over that old frying pan.

I remembered okra, dipped in cornmeal, bubbling in all its fragrance, and pies fried golden brown, filled with peaches from our orchard. Mother served these right from the skillet to our waiting plates, topped with plenty of warm melted butter. I remembered the long family dining table, always covered with one of Mother's homemade linen tablecloths, where we sat together each day at mealtimes.

Fifty years later I still use this skillet, and each time I use it I remember those who have used it before me, and those who have benefitted from its service. I think of my mother and my father and my brothers and sisters, all of us brought together over meals that began in this simple iron pan.

Yes, I wanted that skillet. And someday I will pass it along to my own son, as part of his heritage, and as a reminder of other times, other places, and other people.

REFLECTIONS OF HOME

Laurie Wilcox

An open fire, an easy chair,
My sewing basket sitting there,
A reading lamp that's always near,
To send forth rays of warmth and cheer.

The cozy feeling that comes o'er
When first I open the wide door,
To a room that is my very own,
A part of me and me alone.

The flowers that I picked myself,
My glasses on the corner shelf,
A book I love within hand's reach,
My favorite fruits, a bowl for each.

My kitchen with its fragrant air,
A well-worn high-backed rocking chair,
No matter where I move or roam,
My hands can always make a home.

Photo Opposite
Jessie Walker, Photographer

50 YEARS AGO

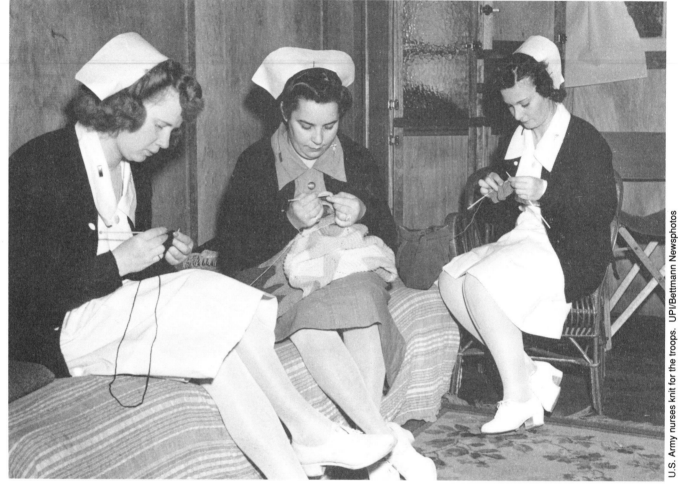

U.S. Army nurses knit for the troops.   UPI/Bettmann Newsphotos

Knitters—Plain, Fancy, or Otherwise

The American Red Cross announced recently that if everything goes as expected, by the first of September the knitters of America will have transformed 157,075 pounds of yarn into warm clothing for war refugees. This is in line with an established tradition. Every war makes knitting a fashionable pursuit. The men hardly have time to grab their guns before their wives and sweethearts grab needles and yarn.

The Red Cross has an arrangement whereby skilled knitters are supplied with wool—colored navy blue, oxford gray, and maroon—and set to plying needles for beleaguered citizens. Theoretically the products go to the civilians of all countries, although Germany has rather awkwardly refrained from asking for a share. Any one who wishes her sweaters sent to a specific country may arrange it that way if she is willing to pay for the wool herself. Organizations like "Bundles for Britain" sell wool at cost to be knitted for British soldiers.

A woman displays her knitting to two American soldiers. UPI/Bettmann Newsphotos

If this war had broken out a decade ago, the Red Cross might have been less sanguine about meeting its 157, 075-pound quota. In the past few years knitting has become increasingly popular. Since 1937 it has been one of the ranking feminine hobbies, even competing with bridge. In 1914-18 there were plenty of jokes about the ineptness of the amateur knitter, but now people are taking a slightly different tack. A few months ago *Punch* ran a cartoon showing a Tommy trying on a sweater made for him by a loved one at home. It was a perfectly competently made sweater—only it was short, with a nipped-in waist and cunning little puffed sleeves. The caption ran: "It's the only kind she knows how to make."

Knitting requires very little apprenticeship. A beginner can start right in making something. Instructors recommend beginning on a simple object like a scarf, but if that seems too dull, they say that skirts, once they are properly launched, are easy to do. Most beginners automatically want to do sweaters, but this is discouraged because a well-fitting sweater is fairly tough going.

But no matter what they are working on, women who knit are likely to have the same comfortable expression—interested and relaxed. The quick, automatic movement of the fingers absorbs their restlessness and the soft steady click of the needles is soothing to hear. They like the quiet touch of the wool sliding over their fingers. They get a satisfaction from the orderly rows of stitches falling into patterns of accomplishment. In times like these there are few occupations that have this sort of effect. It is possible that women in wartime knit as much for the knitting itself as for what their knitting accomplishes.

Copyright © 1940 by The New York Times Company. Reprinted by permission.

HER HOME

Alice B. Dorland

Her home's a charming place,
I declare.
It has friendly warmth and light.
It has an air
Of being lived in, being loved.
Every picture, lamp, and chair
Seems to speak of her great care.

Her dining table, old and treasured,
Softly gleams.
Her fine old Highboy stands at ease,
So it seems.
It communes with fragile china,
Polished glass and shining silver,
As it dreams.

Her home is a charming place,
I declare.
It has warmth and peace.
It has an air
Of being lived in, being loved.
Every picture, book, and chair
Seems to bid you welcome there.

Photo Opposite
Jessie Walker, Photographer

LEGENDARY AMERICANS

Anne Bradstreet

verses from "Upon the Burning of Our House" by Anne Bradstreet

In silent night when rest I took
For sorrow near I did not look
I waken'd was with thundering noise
And piteous shrieks of dreadful voice.
That fearful sound of fire and fire,
Let no man know is my desire.

I, starting up, the light did spy,
And to my God my heart did cry
To strengthen me in my distress
And not to leave me succorless.
Then coming out beheld a space,
The flame consume my dwelling place.

Here stood that trunk, and there that chest;
There lay that store I counted best:
My pleasant things in ashes lie,
And them behold no more shall I.
Under thy roof no guest shall sit,
Nor at thy table eat a bit.

No pleasant tale shall 'ere be told,
Nor things recounted done of old.
No candle 'ere shall shine in thee,
Nor bridegroom's voice 'ere heard shall be.
In silence ever shall thou lie;
Adieu, Adieu; All's vanity.

Thou hast an house on high erect,
Fram'd by that mighty Architect,
With glory richly furnished,
Stands permanent though this be fled.
It's purchased and paid for too
By him who hath enough to do.

A prize so vast as is unknown,
Yet by his gift is made thine own.
There's wealth enough, I need no more;
Farewell my pelf, farewell my store.
The world no longer let me love,
My hope and treasure lies above.

On July 10, 1666, fire destroyed the North Andover, Massachusetts, house that Anne and Simon Bradstreet had built together for themselves and their children. As Mrs. Bradstreet looked on, her heart rose in anger and frustration; she was helpless as the flames consumed the possessions of a lifetime. But when she sat down later to put her thoughts to paper, the verses that our first great American poet wrote upon the burning of her house were not verses of despair. They were, and they remain, verses of hope and inspiration.

It was necessarily a faith well-tested that allowed Anne Bradstreet to find this consolation on that long-ago summer night. For this was not an ordinary house. This was a house built thousands of miles and one wide ocean away from its roots, a house built on foreign soil in a harsh and unwelcoming wilderness—a house that must, nonetheless, be the foundation of a new home.

And the foundation of a new country, for the Bradstreet home was a part of the first Puritan settlement of Massachusetts. They came seeking a haven from the corruption and persecution they saw threatening the church in England. But they were not merely running away, they were determined to found a new outpost of civilization, an example of religious purity for the world to follow. This was a group with a powerful sense of mission. Simon Bradstreet was an assistant in John Winthrop's Massachusetts Bay Company, and Anne's father, Thomas Dudley, would eventually be elected deputy governor. And to eighteen-year-old Anne Bradstreet and the other women of the group fell the responsibility of setting down roots and making New England home.

What an incredible leap of faith this must have required for a girl of Anne's age, pious but untested. She left behind in England a comfortable life; a beautiful home, an affluent family, and an access to education generally unheard of for girls of her day. She left all this for the severity and isolation of New England, for the challenge of building a life from scratch.

How was a young girl to accept such an upheaval, to meet this challenge with no model to guide her? The answer is revealed in the poetry that she wrote throughout her life. In her earliest work, she displays great skill and intelligence, but the verses are stiff and dated, notable today only as relics of our history. This is not surprising. As a girl Bradstreet studied the works of the Puritan poets of her day, and was naturally intimidated and could not feel the confidence in her own voice necessary for true poetic creation. She relied, rather, on skillful imitation. Yet when she arrived on the shores of New England her old models began to fade from her memory; and as they disappeared, they left a void that she must either fill with her own self-confident voice or allow to silence her completely.

In the face of this void, Bradstreet turned to what she knew best. She took the role assigned to her and made it a powerful one; she made home-building the subject of her poetry and the work of her lifetime. Her poems now concerned her children—her fears for their survival, her devotion to their well-being, and her hopes for their salvation. She wrote also of her husband—the absences that kept him away and the bonds that held them together. As time passed, Bradstreet let go of the England of her childhood and embraced New England, both the physical beauty of its wilderness and the inner life that its isolation fostered. She became a truly American poet—our first and one of our most accomplished.

This shift in poetic focus is the reflection of a developing personal focus. Bradstreet's challenge was to build a home in a new world, and she met that challenge with an acceptance of God's unfailing guidance and a commitment to home and family. Bradstreet's poetry is not limited by the tenets of her faith, nor is it confined by the boundaries of the seventeenth century. Like all great poetry, it is timeless. The power of Bradstreet's verses is the power of the woman who accepted God's will without being crushed by its weight, and found in that acceptance the strength to rise to any occasion.

Thus, as Anne Bradstreet's house burned to the ground, taking with it all the material goods she and her family had accumulated, she did not despair. Rather, she took her pen and set about rebuilding immediately, with the self-confident voice that speaks from a powerful and unquestioning commitment to the strength of one's own personal faith and provides a model of home-building for the nation she helped found.

Nancy Skarmeas

Photo Overleaf
Country Church
Wisconsin
Ken Dequaine Photography

My Heart
Can Understand

Carol Besset Hayman

I do not wish to gather
    fame or fortune,
I am content with what
    each morning brings.
My place in life is small
    and not noteworthy,
I'm happiest among
    the quiet things.

The garden swing at twilight
    is my blessing,
The smell of roses and
    the song of birds . . .

The pines against the evening sky
    are patterned
In colors far too
    beautiful for words.

My house is warm
    with friends and filled with music,
A favorite book
    is always close at hand,
A cup of tea, an open fire . . .
    day-dreaming . . .
These are the things
    my heart can understand.

70

Where the Heart Is

Carice Williams

What made the humble cottage seem
    so loving to the heart?
Was it because the roses red
    their fragrance did impart?
Was it because a friendly fire
    made all seem warm and fair?
No it was because of the loving heart
    ever dwelling there.

What made it seem like heaven was near
    when evening shadows fell
And we would sit at Mother's knee
    and listen to her tell

The stories of a magic world
    that seemed so far away—
What I would give to live again
    those scenes of yesterday.

Yes, home is where the heart is found
    in castle or in shack,
And where in spite of journeying
    we always do go back.
Home is where a loved one's smile
    puts heaven a step away,
Yes home is where all footsteps turn
    at the closing of the day.

And unto Thee
Our Lives in Purity

Caroline Eyring Miner

Today we dedicate this house to Thee,
Dear Lord, this glorious chapel we have built,
Its spire, a finger lifted reverently
Toward Thee whose precious blood was freely spilled
For us. It is the symbol of our love,
Our unity, our hope of better things;
Our faith in leaders with a dream above
Self-interest, whose fulfillment brings
A satisfaction known alone to those
Who act as loving shepherds to the fold
Leading aright their precious flocks to enclose
Them in a sheltered haven where no cold,
No unbelief, no hurt, nor harm can come.

From this day on let quiet peace be here!
Let there be tolerance for all; let some
Sweet music, gracious deed, kind word of cheer,
Given some lonely heart within this place,
Lead him to look with joy upon Thy face.
Let there be faith and hope and charity,
No discord, only joyous harmony.
Today we dedicate this house to Thee,
And unto Thee our lives in purity.

Camden, Maine
Suzanne Clemenz Photography

That Makes a House a Home

Garnett Ann Schultz

It isn't curtains starched and fine
Nor windows shining clean,
Expensive paintings on the walls
That catch the sunlight's gleam,

Nor furniture so new and grand
The many things you own,
For not a single one of these
Can make a house a home.

It matters not a speck of dust
To real folks this won't count,
Nor that you have the worldly things
In any large amount,
A house can never be a home
However hard you'd try,
Unless the welcome's friendly there—
A twinkle in your eye.

It takes a handshake firm and true
A greeting warm and gay,
An air of love and happiness
As we would go our way,

'Tis these that make a house a home
Though worldy things are few,
And folks will always come again
But just because of you.

A house can never be a home
However long we live,
Unless it's filled with friendliness
With laughter we can give,
Whatever else we chance to have
How much we gain or own,
'Tis only people real and true
That make a house a home.

FOR THOSE WHO HAVE NO PLACE TO GO

Betty W. Stoffel

Lord, in Thy mercy's tender care
Hear an urgent, earnest prayer
For all who wander to and fro
And have no special place to go.

Who see the windows warm with light
In other people's homes at night,
And feel their loneliness the more
That others hurry to some door
Where love expectant warms the air,
And one is loved by those who care.

Bless those who rootless, restless roam
And have no place to be at home;
Remember those we may not know
Who have no special place to go.

Photo Opposite
Portland Head Lighthouse
Cape Elizabeth, Maine
Jeff Gnass Photography

Readers' Forum

Ideals *has become a treasured friend here at the John B. Parsons Home in Salisbury, Maryland. The beautiful poems and inspiring prayers are so well received by the Parsons residents. Ideals is used cover to cover during our reading activities. Thank you for providing such beautiful literature!*

Pat English
Salisbury, Maryland

I love my Ideals *magazines,*
The poems, articles, and beautiful scenes.
I would like to keep each and every one
But that is something that can't be done.
So I share them with relatives and friends,
Even though my heart it fairly rends.
Still, there are some with which I cannot part,
And when I look through them again,
They soothe my aching heart.

Phyllis Wand
Freeport, Illinois

For years I have been a regular subscriber to Ideals *and enjoy every issue. The poetry is inspirational and the photography breathtaking. The two roses on the cover of your February issue, and the pictures of Lincoln, were so realistic that I had to frame them. I pass each issue on and those who read it enjoy every picture and poem as much as I do. We are all Delaware natives or residents, which leads me to make a very important point. Seldom, if ever, have I seen a photo of a scene in Delaware, and though we are a very small state, we do have some lovely spots . . . just because we are little doesn't mean we don't enjoy seeing ourselves in print occasionally. Thank you!*

Helen G. Clapp
Wilmington, Delaware

Ed: In our Easter 1990 issue we did include a photo of Delaware. Our photo caption, however, mistakenly located the flowering cherry tree in Josephine Gardens on page 13 in Wilmington, Virginia. In truth, the tree is located in the small but beautiful state of Delaware, in Wilmington's Josephine Gardens. We apologize for our error.

Editor's Note: Readers are invited to submit unpublished, original poetry, short anecdotes, and humorous reflections on life for possible publication in future *Ideals* issues. Please send copies only; manuscripts will not be returned. Writers receive $10 for each published submission. Send material to "Readers' Reflections," Ideals Publishing Corporation, P. O. Box 140300, Nashville, Tennessee, 37214-0300.

I have searched for a number of years for poems, etc, about birthdays. I think it would be a lovely idea for your publication. I can just see some of the lovely art work, birthday cakes, and family gatherings centered around such a special celebration. How about it? Ideals *is pure joy and beauty!*

Mary Ella Fitzpatrick
Lebanon, Tennessee

My grandmother receives your magazine and ever since I was a little girl I always looked at the pictures and thought they were so beautiful. As I got older and sat down to read the articles I enjoyed them very much. My two-year-old daughter looks at them already and I know where mine will go one day. Thank you for making so many people happy!

Valerie K. McFadden
Millersburg, Ohio

Congratulations to your company for the lovely Easter Ideals. *It is so inspirational in words, pictures, thoughts, and feelings of truthful glory within one's heart and soul. It was indeed a pleasure to read and reread and pass on to others in this nursing home . . . I lend my magazine to so many who are discouraged to bring them true joys that can be found from God's own creative beauty here on earth . . .*

Ruth S. Hinterberg
Mooretown, New Jersey

I now have all my Ideals *in binders or slipcases. One thing I have done is mark them Christmas, Valentine, Easter, Mother's Day, Thanksgiving, and the odd ones as miscellaneous. So whatever the season I bring down that binder on my coffee table and people who come to my house enjoy them.*

Mrs. James J. (Dorothy) Dix
Elm Grove, Wisconsin

Want to share your crafts?
Readers are invited to submit original craft ideas for possible development and publication in future Ideals *issues. Please send query letter (with photograph, if possible) to Editorial Features Department, Ideals Publishing Corporation, P.O. Box 140300, Nashville, Tennessee 37214-0300. Please do not send craft samples; they cannot be returned.*

AN OPPORTUNITY TO COMPLETE YOUR COLLECTION OF IDEALS MAGAZINE!

Here is your once-a-year opportunity to complete your collection of the beautiful and seasonal *Ideals!* Many of our reade, request particular issues, but only a few of a limited number of issues are available. Order now, either by phone and credit car or send us a check at the special price of $3.00 for each book ordered. Postage will be paid by us.

I10516A   **Mother's Day**   **1987**
American Crossroads visits Indiana Parke County, "I Love Dandelions" by Carol Hammond, "Feathering Her Own Nest" by Elizabeth Thom, and poetic tributes to Mom.

I10524A   **Countryside**   **1987**
One of our favorites combining the patriotic with the beauty of the land; "The Country Inside" by Pam Kennedy, "Blessings of Liberty," and "The Trail West" by Joy Belle Burgess.

I10540A   **Autumn**   **1987**
Brilliant photography from the most beautiful season of the year, "Hearty Autumn Soups," "The Last Leaf" by Pam Kennedy, and "Country Chronicle" goes in search of hickory nuts.

I10559A   **Thanksgiving**   **1987**
"A Step into the Past," "Other Thanksgivings" by Pam Kennedy, "The Lost Colony" of Roanoke, "Thanksgiving Time" by Laura Ingalls Wilder, and beautiful scenics of Autumn.

I10567A   **Christmas**   **1987**
"Home for Christmas" by Laura Ingalls Wilder, "A Winter Walk" by Henry Thoreau, recipes for German Stollen and Holiday Wreath Pie, "The Second Christmas" by Pam Kennedy, and spectacular photos of the season.

I10591A   **Valentine**   **1988**
"Sawdust and Dreams" by Edgar A. Guest, Collector's Corner on Old-Fashioned Valentines, directions for making heart sachets and garlands, and, "An American Valentine" by Pam Kennedy.

I10605A   **Easter**   **1988**
Collector's Corner features bisque and china dolls, directions for making an applique Bible cover, "He Is Risen Indeed" by Pam Kennedy, and "Relics of an Old World Easter" by Walter Wentz.

I10613A   **Mother's Day**   **1988**
"A Thousand Million Questions" by Phyllis Michael, "Once a Mother, Always a Mother" by Pam Kennedy, "Mother's Day" by Edgar A. Guest, and directions for making Applique Rose Pillows.

I10621A   **Summertime**   **1988**
Collector's Corner looks at old postcards, make rose potpourri from backyard roses, "Salute to the Statue of Liberty," applique a barbecue apron, and gorgeous scenery from around the nation.

I1063XA   **Old Fashioned**   **1988**
Old photographs, "The Shaker Message," Carnival Glass from a collector's viewpoint, directions for picnic cloth and napkins, and "Something Old" by Pam Kennedy.

I10648A   **Autumn**   **1988**
Opening spread is the beautiful "Birches" by Robert Frost, Collector's Corner features old U.S. coins, recipes for autumn casseroles, Pam Kennedy's "Reflections," and directions for a cross-stitch glass case.

I10656A   **Thanksgiving**   **1988**
"A Time for Settling In" by Carol McCray, applique a Pilgrim potholder, Collector's Corner looks at antique clocks, and Pam Kennedy's "A Letter Home" from a might-have-been adventurer.

I10664A   **Christmas**   **1988**
"Keeping Christmas" by Henry Van Dyke, "The Twenty-Sixth of December" by Donald Stoltz, directions for Patchwork Stockings, Collector's Corner featuring Electric Trains, The Story of the Birth of Christ from Luke 2, and the beauty of the season in photography.

I10699A   **Valentine**   **1989**
Featuring articles on "Phoenix Bird" pattern china, "Down Life Stream" by Margaret Sangster, Craftworks featuring Decoupage, a love poetry befitting the season.

I10702A   **Easter**   **1989**
The religious Easter Story, directions for decorative sugar eggs, Pam Kennedy's fictional account of Simon meeting the Messiah, Collector's Corner featuring miniatures, and breathtaking photos of the flowers of spring.

I10737A   **Mother's Day**   **1989**
Norman Rockwell's Collectibles are featured, the planting and ca of lilacs discussed, "My Cinderella Grandmother" by Kathle Gilbert, recipes for strawberry torte and other delights, and directio for pressed flower notes.

I10745A   **Country**   **1989**
Garden Journal features the daylily, "My Birthday" by Ray Koonce, "How Does She Do It?" by Linda Massen, "Tomfoolery" by Gail Wyatt, "What Makes a Nation Great?" and Pam Kennedy's article on the memorial Arizona.

I10753A   **Home**   **1989**
Garden Journal shows you how to plant a "Cutting Garden," "Country Chronicle" takes a walk and listens to the sounds of the country side, directions for applique sweatshirts, and "Martha's Home" Cynthia Wyatt.

I10761A   **Friendship**   **1989**
"Drying Herbs" by Gladys Taber, Garden Journal plants late-blooming flowers, directions for personalizing picture frames, Pam Kennedy's "Friends for All Seasons," and "The One-Room Schoolhouse" by Talbert Pond.

I1077XA   **Thanksgiving**   **1989**
Features the history and the beauty of the season for the whole family, grow a sweet potato houseplant, "Let's Be Thankful" by Ma Reiter, "The First Feast" by Jane Austin, and "Giving Thanks" Joy Ward.

I10788A   **Christmas**   **1989**
Directions for making felt ornaments for the tree, "A Stable Boy's Christmas" by Pam Kennedy, "Luke, the Man Who Gave Us Christmas," "Christmas in America" by Angela Hunt, and "Let Us Keep Christmas" by Grace Noll Crowell.

TO ORDER:
Include your name, title, date, and order number of the books you want, plus a check or money order.

CALL TOLL FREE 1-800-558-4343 to order by credit card. Or send check or money order to:

IDEALS COLLECTIBLES
P.O. Box 148000
Nashville, TN 37214-8000